### Our Amazing World

# TIGERS

Kay de Silva

*Aurora*

# Contents

| | | | | |
|---|---|---|---|---|
| Tigers | 5 | Tiger Cubs | 19 |
| Anatomy | 7 | Bengal Tigers | 21 |
| Habitat | 9 | Indochinese Tigers | 23 |
| Camouflage | 10 | Malayan Tigers | 24 |
| Eyesight | 11 | Siberian Tigers | 25 |
| Smell | 13 | South China Tigers | 26 |
| Roaring | 14 | Sumatran Tigers | 27 |
| Swimming | 15 | White Tigers | 29 |
| Territory | 16 | Ligers & Tigons | 31 |
| Diet | 17 | Protect the Tigers | 32 |
| Hunting | 18 | | |

*A prowling tiger.*

# TIGERS

Tigers are *mammals* that belong to the cat family. They are the largest of all cats. These magnificent creatures have roamed the earth for about 2 million years.

# ANATOMY

Tigers are built to be ferocious predators. Adult tigers can be about 11 feet (3 meters) in length. They weigh about 670 pounds (300 kilograms). They have large heads, muscular bodies, and powerful legs, which help them take down prey many times larger and heavier than themselves.

*A tiger in motion: strong, swift, and magnificent.*

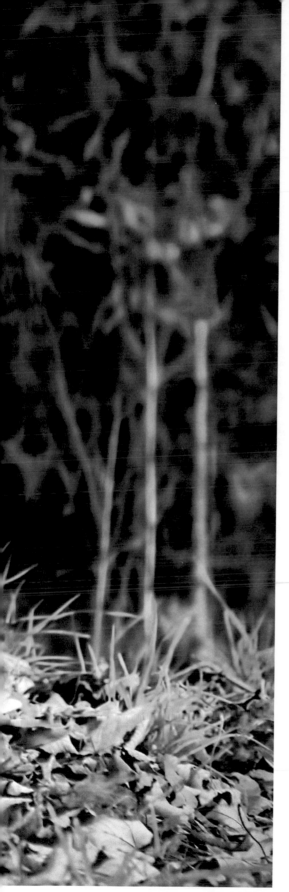

# Habitat

Tigers are found in a range of habitats in Asia and Far-East Russia. Different types of tigers are found in different habitats. These include rainforests, swamps, and grasslands.

All tigers need dense *vegetation*—that is, lots of trees, bushes, and tall grasses. They also need plenty of food and water to survive.

*A rare sighting of a Sumatran Tiger Cub.*

*A perfectly camouflaged Malayan Tiger peering through the brush.*

# CAMOUFLAGE

Tigers are easily recognized by the stripes on their bodies. Most tigers have over 100 stripes. The striped pattern is also found on tigers' skins, so even if a tiger were shaved, the pattern would still be visible.

The patterns of tiger stripes are *unique*. This means that no two tigers will ever have the same striped pattern. Just like human fingerprints are used to identify humans, tigers' coats are used to identify them.

Tigers' markings also help them to *camouflage* or blend in with their surroundings. These markings are useful in hiding from their predators and also help when sneaking up on prey.

*Close up of a Tiger's eyes.*

# EYESIGHT

Tigers have the brightest eyes in the world. Their eyes have a mirror-like structure, which allows unabsorbed light back into the eye to produce a brighter image. This is what causes cat eyes to blaze back when light is directly shone at them.

They also have good day and night vision. Their day vision is as sharp as a human's. Their *visual acuity*, or ability see in detail, is not as good. At night, however, when they usually hunt, their eyesight is six times better than a human's.

# SMELL

Tigers have an excellent sense of smell. They, however, rarely use this sense for hunting. They use their sense of smell mainly to communicate with other tigers.

When smelling another tigers' scent marks, tigers wrinkle their noses and hang out their tongues in a grimace called *flehmen*. Flehmen is used to draw the scent to the Jacobson's organ located in the roof of their mouth. This organ receives *chemical information*. In this way, tigers can sense whether the scent belongs to a local tiger or a stranger and whether the other tiger is male or female.

*A Bengal Tiger investigating its environment.*

*Beware the roaring tiger.*

# ROARING

A tiger is known as a *Big Cat*, not just because of its size, but also because of its ability to roar. Other Big Cats include the Lion, Jaguar, and Leopard. Tigers do not always roar to show *aggression* or anger. Tigers also growl, hiss, and moan.

Tigers are able to make sounds below the human range of hearing. This is called *infrasound*. These sounds can travel across long distances and pass through solid objects, including dense forests and mountains.

Using infrasound, Tigers are known to *paralyze* their prey or stop them in their tracks. These sounds are so powerful that even though you may not hear the sound, you could *feel* it in your bones.

*A Siberian Tiger hunting underwater.*

# SWIMMING

Tigers love water. They are often found bathing in rivers, lakes, and ponds. They are powerful swimmers. They can cross rivers of up to 5 miles (7 km) wide. They can also swim up to about 18 miles (30 km) a day. Of all the Big Cats, only the Jaguar shares the tiger's love for and abilities in the water.

Tigers dislike the heat, so they like to spend time cooling off in the water. Most Tigers will soak in water after making a kill. They may also capture their prey in the water.

*A Tiger fiercely guarding its territory.*

# TERRITORY

A group of tigers is known as an *ambush* or a *streak*. Finding a group of tigers is rare, as tigers are usually solitary animals. This means that they like to live alone.A tiger finds a *territory* or space that it considers its own and will guard it from other tigers.

Tigers are often found patrolling and marking their territories. They do this by spraying *urine* on bushes, trees, and rocks. In addition to leaving this foul smell, they also leave scratch marks on trees and on the ground.

*A tiger tucking into a meal.*

# Diet

Tigers mainly eat large mammals. Their favourite food is *ungulates* or hooved animals such as deer and wild boar. They sometimes eat smaller mammals and birds. Tigers also eat crocodiles, fish, reptiles, and other predators such as bears and leopards.

Tigers are big eaters. They can eat 100 pounds (45 kilograms) of meat a night. This is as much as 400 hamburgers! After getting their fill, tigers cover the *carcass* or dead animal's remains with dirt. They return over several days to the *kill* to eat the rest.

*A tiger stealthily stalking its prey.*

# HUNTING

Tigers are keen hunters. They prefer to hunt at night. They rely mainly on their senses of sight and sound, rather than smell. These solitary hunters carefully stalk their prey and sneak up to it as close as possible. Then they sprint to the unsuspecting animals, usually pulling them off their feet, using their teeth and claws. Locking their jaws around the neck of their prey, tigers strangle their victims to death.

*A mother tiger giving her cub a ride.*

# TIGER CUBS

Baby tigers are called *cubs*. A female tiger usually gives birth to 2-7 cubs. A group of cubs is called a *litter*.

Tiger cubs are born blind and helpless. After ten days or so a baby tiger opens its blue eyes for the first time. Like all mammals, newborn cubs depend entirely on their mother for food and protection. For the first 6-8 weeks they drink only their mother's milk.

As they get older, their mother takes them out to kills to feed. There are scent glands between tigers' toes that leave a unique scent. This enables cubs to follow their mother's *pug marks* or paw prints.

# BENGAL TIGERS

*Bengal Tigers* are also known as *Indian Tigers*. They are found in India, Bangladesh, Bhutan, Nepal, and Burma. From the chilly Himalayan forests, to the hot swamps and wet forests of North India, to the dry forests of Rajasthan, this is the most common species or type of tiger found in the wild.

Bengal Tigers eat boars, wild oxen, and monkeys. They prefer to eat young or old animals because they do not run very fast.

*A Royal Bengal Tiger staring at the camera.*

# INDOCHINESE TIGERS

*Indochinese Tigers* are also known as *Corbett's Tigers*. They are found in Thailand, Vietnam, Laos, Burma, and Cambodia. They used to be found in China, but are now believed to be extinct in the wild in that part of the world.

Finding these tigers is difficult, as they live high up in the mountains in lonely forest areas. For this reason not much is known about these tigers. They are often mistaken for Bengal Tigers. If you take a close look at their stripes, however, you will notice that they are quite narrow compared to other tiger species.

Their primary prey includes antelope, buffalo, deer, and wild boar. They may also eat elephants, monkeys, baby rhinoceroses, birds, fish, and turtles. When food is scarce, they will eat whatever they can find.

*An Indochinese Tiger playing with her cub.*

*A close-up of a Malayan Tiger.*

# MALAYAN TIGERS

*Malayan Tigers* or Malay Tigers are found only on the Malayan Peninsula, which includes Thailand and Malaysia. The beautiful tropical and sub-tropical broadleaf forests are ideal habitats for Malayan Tigers.

Malayan Tigers have various food sources. These include the sun bear, wild boars, and deer. They will feed on smaller animals, if they cannot find their usual prey. The smaller prey, however, do not give them enough energy needed for survival.

*A Siberian Tiger in its natural habitat.*

# SIBERIAN TIGERS

*Siberian Tigers* are also known as *Amur Tigers*. They live mainly in Russia's birch forests and are also found in China and North Korea. Siberian Tigers are one of the world's largest cats. Their skins are of a lighter pallor than other tigers. This helps them to blend in with their snowy habitat.

These tigers mainly eat deer, musk, hare, and salmon. Apart from this prey, Siberian Tigers sometimes attack larger animals such as brown bears. These bears, however, are known to kill tigers to defend themselves or to take revenge.

*A rare sighting of the critically endangered South China Tiger.*

# SOUTH CHINA TIGERS

*South China Tigers* are also known as Chinese, Amoy, or Xiamen Tigers. They are found in Central and Eastern China. This area used to be occupied by Siberian, Indochinese, and Bengal Tigers, too, but they are no longer found there.

South China Tigers prefer thick jungles and love to spend time in the water. These tigers are recognised by their coats, which have broad stripes, spaced farther apart compared to other tigers.

Like most tigers, South China Tigers prefer medium and large-sized prey. When food is scant, however, they will eat almost any other animal. Common prey includes birds, monkeys, and small bucks.

*Sumatran Tiger cubs playing on the forest floor.*

# SUMATRAN TIGERS

*Sumatran Tigers* are found only on the Indonesian island of Sumatra. They live in low land, mountain, and peat moss forests.

They are the smallest tigers in the world. Their size allows them to move quickly in the forest. They have thinner stripes than other tigers and sport a beard. Webbing between their toes makes them very fast swimmers.

Sumatran Tigers prey on small animals such as birds and fish. They also enjoy large ungulates such as deer, wild boar, and tapir.

# WHITE TIGERS

*White Tigers* are not a separate *sub-species* or type of tiger. They simply are a rare form of Bengal Tiger. Their unique white coat, blue eyes, and pink nose give them an air of beauty and mystery.

They also stand out from other tigers that are usually orange. White Tigers come with two distinct markings. *Royal White Bengal Tigers* are white with black stripes. *Snow White Bengal Tigers* are all white or have ghost stripes.

Their coloring, however, means that they are poorly camouflaged. This makes them an easy target in the wild. This is one of the reasons that white tigers have short lives.

*A profile of a beautiful White Tiger.*

# LIGERS & TIGONS

*Ligers* are the *offspring* of a father lion and a mother tiger. Ligers are the world's largest cats. They grow up to be larger than their parents. A male liger stands about 12 feet (3.5 meters) tall and weighs about half a ton. This is twice the weight of a wild lion or tiger.

The pairing of a father tiger and mother lion results in a *Tigon*. Tigons are smaller than lions or tigers. Usually bred in captivity, ligers and tigons are rarely found in the wild.

*Liger nursing her cub in Novosibirsk Zoo, Russia.*

*A tiger resting at sunset.*

# PROTECT THE TIGERS

Many tigers are either *endangered* or already extinct. Sadly, they are hunted by humans for their *pelts* or skin for decoration, their bones for medicine, and for sport. They are also losing their habitats and prey because of other human activity.

Sumatran Tigers, for instance, are known as *critically endangered*. Today there are only 400 of these tigers found in nature. South China Tigers are among ten of the most endangered animals in the world. There are just 10-30 of these animals in the wild today.

Being aware of these problems and spreading the word can save these glorious animals from being lost to the world forever.

# OUR AMAZING WORLD
## COLLECT THEM ALL

### WWW.OURAMAZINGWORLDBOOKS.COM

Aurora
An imprint of CKTY Publishing Solutions

www.ouramazingworldbooks.com

71977391R00020